How to Make Grammar Fun— (and Easy!)

by Elizabeth A. Ryan

Troll Associates

Library of Congress Cataloging-in-Publication Data

Ryan, Elizabeth A. (Elizabeth Anne), (date)
  How to make grammar fun—(and easy!) / by Elizabeth A. Ryan.
    p.   cm.—(Student survival power)
  Summary: Discusses such aspects of grammar as the parts of speech,
verb tenses, types of sentences, punctuation, and capitalization.
  ISBN 0-8167-2456-3 (lib. bdg.)   ISBN 0-8167-2457-1 (pbk.)
  1. English language—Grammar—1950—Juvenile literature.
[1. English language—Grammar.] I. Title. II. Series.
PE1112.R93 1992
428—dc20   91-12525

Contents

Introduction:
How This Book Can Help You
(Why Grammar Seems So Hard)

Believe it or not, you already know quite a lot about grammar. For example, can you tell the difference between these two sentences?

Wilbur ate the lobster.

The lobster ate Wilbur.

Both sentences use exactly the same words. Yet the way the words are put together makes a big difference in what they mean. *Grammar* is no more than the structure of a language, the way to put words together in order to make sense. If you can tell the difference between those two sentences, you already know a good deal about English grammar.

When it comes to talking and making yourself understood, you probably don't have any trouble. When you talk, you have your tone of voice and the expression on your face to help your listener understand you. Everyday conversation does not require you to follow a set of formal rules. However, there is a basic set of formal rules for writing (although these ''rules'' have a lot of exceptions and variations, and they keep changing). The grammar for both speaking and writing that fits this uniform set of rules is known as Standard English.

Nobody is born knowing how to speak and write Standard English, just as nobody is born knowing how to talk. You can learn to follow the rules of Standard English grammar just as you learned to talk—by practice and by getting a feel for what sounds right. Just as you know the difference between "Wilbur ate the lobster" and "The lobster ate Wilbur," you can learn the difference between what is and is not correct in Standard English. This book can help you learn.

Part I: THE EIGHT PARTS OF SPEECH
(The Building Blocks)

A word follows different rules, depending on how it is used in the sentence. *Part of speech* is the name for how a word is used in a sentence. There are eight parts of speech: *noun, pronoun, verb, adjective, adverb, preposition, conjunction,* and *interjection.*

The same word can be used as a different part of speech in different sentences. For example, the word round has at least five different uses:

Noun: The boxers went five *rounds.*

Adjective: Don't put the square peg in the *round* hole.

Verb: *Round* off the number to the nearest tenth.

Adverb: Wait till the carousel comes *round* again.

Preposition: She'll be coming *round* the mountain when she comes.

6

Part of Speech	Definition	Examples
noun	names a person, place, thing, idea, or quality	singer, Charles, city, Tulsa, school, love, happiness, anger, pizza, records
pronoun	takes the place of a noun	I, me, you, he, she, it, we, they, us, them, her, him, anybody, everyone, everybody, who, what
verb	expresses physical or mental action, being, or state of being	shouts, thought, is, was, wondering, seems, became, turned
adjective	tells more about a noun or pronoun	ridiculous, smart, fourteen, careless, older, pretty
adverb	tells more about a verb, an adjective, or another adverb	slowly, fast, tomorrow, down, very, hardly, so, happily
preposition	shows how a noun or pronoun relates to another part of the sentence	out, behind, in front of, because of, except for, into, around, between
conjunction	connects words or groups of words	and, but, or, because, either ... or, both... and, besides
interjection	expresses a feeling	oh, er, gee, Wow! Hey! Shh!

7

Chapter 1:
Nouns
(The Name of the Game)

Types of Nouns

A *noun* names a person, place, thing, idea, or quality.

A *proper noun* names a specific person, place, or thing; for example, *Pete Rose, Josie, Minnesota, Disneyland.*

A *common noun* refers to a category of people, places, or things; or else to a specific person, place, or thing that is not named; for example, *player, woman, state, playground.*

An *abstract noun* names an idea or a quality; for example, *freedom, friendliness, freshness.*

A *collective noun* is one word that names a group or collection of people, animals, or things; for example, *class, orchestra, herd, flock.*

A *compound noun* is two or more words that together name one person, place, or thing. Sometimes a compound noun is hyphenated, sometimes it is written as one word, and sometimes it is written as two or more separate words. Check your dictionary for the correct spelling of compound nouns, since there is no one rule that tells you how to write them. Some examples of compound nouns are *ice cream, chairperson,* and *mother-in-law.*

How to Form Plural Nouns

Most nouns form their plurals by adding *s*.

hamburger   hamburgers
record   records

However, many nouns form plurals in other ways. There are some basic rules you should follow to form other kinds of plurals. You may have noticed that there are exceptions to every rule! The English language comes from many different languages, and each language's set of rules has found its way into some part of English.

The only way to be absolutely sure of how to form a plural is to memorize the word or check it in your dictionary. However, knowing the following rules should make remembering a little easier:

Kind of Noun	Rule	Examples
Most nouns	Just add *s*.	clock—clocks tape—tapes
Nouns that end in *s, x, z, ch,* or *sh*	Add *es*.	dress—dresses fox—foxes quartz—quartzes hutch—hutches crash—crashes
Nouns that end in vowel + *y*	Just add *s*.	key—keys replay—replays

Kind of Noun	Rule	Examples
Nouns that end in consonant + *y*	Change the *y* to *i* and add *es*.	party—parties cherry—cherries
Proper nouns that end in *y*	Just add *s*.	Ms. Pally—the Pallys Mr. Carey—the Careys
Nouns that end in *o*	*Usually*, just add *s*.	stereo—stereos alto—altos
	However, *sometimes* add *es*. (Check your dictionary!)	tomato—tomatoes hero—heroes
Nouns that end in *f* or *fe*.	*Sometimes*, just add *s*.	cliff—cliffs belief—beliefs safe—safes
	However, *sometimes* change the *f* to *v* and add *es*. (Check your dictionary!)	life—lives calf—calves leaf—leaves knife—knives
Special nouns	Just memorize or check your dictionary.	man—men crisis—crises
Compound nouns written as one word	Add the plural ending to the end of the whole word.	playground—playgrounds bookstore—bookstores

Kind of Noun	Rule	Examples
Compound nouns written with hyphens or as separate words	Add the plural ending to the most important word in the group	mother-in-law— mothers-in-law (*Not* mother-in-laws) hot dog—hot dogs

There are three other types of plurals that you should know about. One is the type that is spelled exactly the same whether it is singular or plural.

Singular: I like that new TV *series.*
Plural: All the new *series* last year were boring.

Then there are the plural forms that have no singular, and the singular forms that sound plural. Don't be confused. You probably know how to use these words when you speak.

Singular Only
news
    The latest *news* is not good.
    (**Not:** The latest news are not good.)
physics
    Physics was my favorite subject last year.
    (**Not:** Physics were my favorite subject last year.)

Plural Only
pants
    My new *pants* are in the closet.
    (**Not:** My new pants is in the closet.)
scissors
    Those *scissors* were not sharp enough.
    (**Not:** That scissors was not sharp enough.)

Possessive Forms of Nouns

The possessive form of a noun is used to show ownership or possession. If you want to show that someone owns something, is related to someone, or is connected to some quality, you will probably use the possessive form to show this relationship. An apostrophe ' + s is used to show possession.

Louis's honesty   Hallie's book
Lisa Smith's house   Jenny's aunt

Sometimes, when it would be awkward to pronounce another s, an apostrophe is used by itself. This happens when two or more s sounds precede the apostrophe.

Sis' car (the car that belongs to Sis)
Moses' law (the law of Moses)
Ramses' palace (the palace of Ramses)

In general, your best guide is to add 's to singular nouns and just plain ' to plural nouns ending in s or es. You may run across some different examples in your reading, but following this rule will generally keep you on the right track.

One Exception

Can you imagine how you form a possessive when two or more people own something? If all of them own the same object, only the last name is possessive. If they own the objects individually, each name is possessive.

Mark and Jason's house (the house where they both live)
Heather's and Beth's shoes (two pairs of shoes)

Chapter 2:
Pronouns
(Send in the Substitutes)

Types of Pronouns

A *pronoun* takes the place of a noun. A *personal pronoun* names specific people or things.

> I, me, my, mine, you, your, yours, he, she, it, him, her, his, hers, its, we, us, our, ours, they, them, their, theirs

> *I* will be leaving shortly.
> *He* is coming with *me.*
> *They* will meet *us* there.

An *intensive pronoun* shows emphasis. A *reflexive pronoun* refers back to the subject.

> myself, yourself, himself, herself, itself, ourselves, yourselves, themselves

> **Intensive:** I *myself* have never heard of a group called "Hubcap and the Four Wheels."
> **Reflexive:** Tom hurt *himself* on that last play.

13

An *interrogative pronoun* is used to ask a question. (To *interrogate* someone means to ask that person questions.)

who   whom
which   what

Who is going to get us our tickets?
Whom did you see on line?
Which party did you attend?
What price must we pay?

A *demonstrative pronoun* is used to point things out or to demonstrate something.

this   these
that   those

This is the place for me!
Those were the last words the king spoke.

An *indefinite pronoun* names a person, thing, or amount that is not specified, that remains indefinite.

any, anybody, anyone, anything, all, each, everyone, everybody, either, enough, nobody, no one, none, nothing, both, several, more, most, much, few, many, less, little, another

Any of those books will help you learn about windsurfing.
None of the explorers found the Northwest Passage.
Enough of that pizza is left to feed an army!

14

Personal Possessive Pronouns

Like nouns, pronouns can show possession. Following are the personal possessive pronouns.

my, mine	our, ours
your, yours	your, yours
his, her, hers, its	their, theirs

However, personal possessive pronouns differ from nouns in one important way. You do not add an 's because they already show possession.

Lenny's jacket	his jacket
the dog's bark	its bark

Its Versus It's

Be careful not to confuse the contraction *it's,* meaning ''it is,'' with the possessive pronoun *its.* If you are not sure which word to use, ask yourself if you can substitute the words *it is.* If you can, use the apostrophe.

It?s going to be a quiet day.

It is going to be a quiet day. (Yes, use apostrophe.)

The team lost *it?s* opening game.

The team lost *it is* opening game. (Wait a minute! No, no apostrophe.)

15

Chapter 3:
Verbs
(Getting the Job Done!)

Understanding Transitive and Intransitive Verbs

A *verb* expresses physical or mental action, being, or state of being; for example, *throw*, *think*, and *seem*. A *transitive verb* is a verb that passes its action on.

Maria *threw* the ball.

She *painted* a pleasant scene.

An *intransitive verb* does not pass its action on.

Josie *slept* soundly as the teacher *talked*.

Harvey *wondered* about the ball game.

Meanwhile, Petunia's little brother *ate* without stopping.

Although words follow these intransitive verbs, they do not receive the action of the verb.

Most verbs can be either transitive or intransitive, depending on how they are used.

Transitive: Maria *dreamed* a beautiful dream.

Intransitive: She *dreamed* about the ball game.

Working with Linking Verbs

A *linking verb* links the subject of a sentence with a word that tells more about the subject.

Teresa *is* a doctor.

She *seems* proud of her job.

She *became* a specialist last year.

Nevertheless, she *feels* happy.

Some Common Linking Verbs
forms of the verb *to be:*
am, is, are, was, were, has been, will be, and so forth
verbs of the senses: tastes, smells, feels, looks, sounds
others: becomes, turns, seems, grows

Remember: Sometimes a verb can be an action verb, and other times it can be a linking verb, depending on how it is used. If a verb connects the subject of the sentence with a word that identifies or describes it, it is a linking verb. If a verb expresses action, it is not a linking verb

Linking verb: Luis *grows* tired after practice.

Transitive action verb: Luis *grows* tomatoes in his garden.

Intransitive action verb: Luis *grows* more slowly than his brother.

A clue: If you can substitute the word *seems* or *is* for the verb, it is probably a linking verb. If you can't make this substitution, the verb is probably an action verb.

Linking: The pizza *is* spicy.

Action: Pedro *tastes* the pizza.

(You couldn't say, ''Pedro *is* the pizza.'')

Chapter 4:
Adjectives
(Describing It)

An *adjective* modifies, or describes, a noun or a pronoun.

    the *red* truck   the *delicious* hamburger

    the *starry* night   the *fantastic* band

An adjective answers the question *what kind, how many,* or *which one.* Adjectives usually come before the nouns or pronouns they modify. Sometimes, however, an adjective will come after a linking verb.

    The *proud* high jumper rested quietly.

    The high jumper was *proud.*

An adjective will also sometimes come right after the noun it modifies, separated only by a comma.

    The high jumper, *proud* and *tired,* rested quietly.

A *proper adjective* is formed from a proper noun or is a proper noun used as an adjective.

    The *Shakespearean* actor spoke his lines flawlessly.

    This year, we have had more *April* showers than usual.

Like proper nouns, proper adjectives are always capitalized.

Chapter 5:
Adverbs
(Telling How, When, and Where)

An *adverb* modifies—tells more about—a verb, an adjective, or another adverb.

flies *quickly*	(*quickly* modifies the verb *flies*)
flies *very* quickly	(*very* modifies the adverb *quickly*)
The plane was *quite* fast.	(*quite* modifies the adjective *fast*)

An adverb answers the question *how, when, where,* or *to what extent.* Adverbs that tell *how* are usually formed by adding *ly* to an adjective.

Adjective: The skater was *graceful.*
Adverb: He circled the rink *gracefully.*
(*How* did he circle the rink? *Gracefully.*)

However, be careful: Not all words that end in *-ly* are adverbs. Some are adjectives.

Adjective: Rita is a *friendly* person.
Adjective: Cyanide is a *deadly* poison.

Remember, adjectives answer the question *what kind, how many,* or *which one.*

19

Adverbs that tell *when, how often,* or *how long* modify verbs.

soon	later	before	sometimes	forever
now	immediately	always	usually	shortly
then	afterward	never	often	already

Let's go to the concert *tonight.*
(*When* should we go? *Tonight.*)
You *always* want to go out!
(*How often* do you want to go out? *Always!*)
But you take *forever* to get ready.
(*How long* do you take? *Forever.*)

Adverbs that tell *to what extent* usually modify adjectives or other adverbs. They are often called *intensifiers* because they make a word more or less intense.

very	almost	extremely	too	less
quite	rather	somewhat	overly	more

We are *extremely* tired.

Some adverbs are used to ask questions: *how, when, where,* and *why.* Still other adverbs tell about a whole sentence, rather than any one word in it.

finally	fortunately	additionally
actually	apparently	anyway
unfortunately	certainly	therefore

Finally, we are studying adverbs.
Actually, I already knew about them.
Unfortunately, I sometimes forget.

20

Chapter 6:
Prepositions
(Pointing Out Relationships)

A *preposition* is a word that shows how a noun or pronoun relates to another part of the sentence.

Petie stood <u>behind the door.</u>

In the sentence above, the preposition, *behind*, is underlined twice. The *prepositional phrase, behind the door,* is underlined once. The preposition relates the noun *door* to another part of the sentence by showing that Petie stood behind it. The preposition helps us to picture the relationship between Petie and the door.

A *prepositional phrase* is made up of a preposition and its *object*. In the sentence above, the word *door* is the object of the preposition.

Following are some more examples of prepositions and how they are used within prepositional phrases.

One-word prepositions:

before class   *in* the movie

after school   *into* the theater

Two-word prepositions:

except for the singer

because of the bass player

Three-word prepositions:

on account of rain

in front of the building

Chapter 7:
Conjunctions
(Joining One Thing With Another)

A *conjunction* connects words or groups of words.
my boyfriend *and* I
We left *because* the show was over.
Either we are having dinner *or* we are going
out to lunch.

A *coordinating conjunction* shows that the parts of
the sentence that it connects are of equal importance.
Coordinating conjunctions include *and, but, or, not,
for, so,* and *yet.*
The King *and* Queen
I was tired, *so* I slept.

Correlative conjunctions also connect sentence parts
of equal importance, but they work in pairs: *not
only...but also; either...or; neither...nor; both...and.*
not only strong *but also* durable
neither too fat *nor* too thin

Subordinating conjunctions show that one part of a
sentence is dependent on another: *until, although,
after, before, while, though, whereas, because, since.*
I will wait *until* the bell rings.
She laughed *before* he gave the punch line.

Chapter 8:
Interjections
(Emotion-Charged Words)

An *interjection* expresses a feeling: *oh, er, uh, gee, Wow! Hey! Shh!*

An interjection may introduce a sentence if it is followed by a comma.

Hey, how are you doing?

Oh, not too bad.

If an interjection expresses an especially strong feeling, it stands alone, followed by an exclamation point.

Hey! Don't touch that dial!

Shh! I don't want you to wake the baby.

Remember: An interjection is not a sentence because it does not have a subject and a predicate—it does not express a complete thought. It stands alone, followed by an exclamation point, to express a feeling. You may feel that one interjection expresses more than several well-chosen words—and you might be right. However, it still would not be considered a sentence.

Part II: THE PARTS OF A SENTENCE
(Pieces of the Puzzle)

Chapter 9:
Subjects
(Who's the Star?)

Simple and Complete Subjects

A *sentence* is a group of words that has a subject and a predicate, and expresses a complete thought. A sentence makes sense standing alone.

We're ordering pizza now.

Do you have the phone number?

Whew, I thought I had lost it.

A *subject* is one of the two main parts of a sentence. The other main part of a sentence is the *predicate*. For more about predicates, see Chapter 10. The subject names the person or thing being talked about.

<u>Johnetta</u> is the fastest swimmer in our school.

The <u>girl</u> in the red suit is Johnetta.

<u>Tired and happy, Johnetta</u> finished her laps.

24

The *simple subject* is the main noun or pronoun being talked about. The *complete subject* includes all the adjectives, conjunctions, prepositions, adverbs, and other descriptive words that tell about the subject. In the sentences above, the complete subject is underlined once, and the simple subject is underlined twice.

Subject-Verb Agreement

In Standard English, there is a special way that subjects and verbs are supposed to *agree*, or match. Different verb endings show that verbs belong with different subjects. Following is an example of how most verbs should end in order to agree with different types of subjects.

	Singular	*Plural*
First person:	I *want*	we *want*
Second person:	you *want*	you *want*
Third person:	he, she, it dog, cat, guitar, person *wants*	they dogs, cats, guitars, persons *want*

Remember: *First person* refers to the person speaking. *Second person* is the person spoken to. *Third* person is the person, place, or thing spoken about. *Singular* means one person, place, or thing; *plural* means more than one person, place, or thing.

In the chart above, every verb is in its basic form except for the third-person singular, which adds an *s*. This pattern is kept by all *regular* verbs. *Irregular* verbs have different types of patterns, which must be memorized.

Some Irregular Verbs:

	Singular	*Plural*
First person:	I *am*	we *are*
	I *do*	we *do*
	I *have*	we *have*
Second person:	you *are*	you *are*
	you *do*	you *do*
	you *have*	you *have*
Third person:	he, she, it *is*	they *are*
	does	*do*
	has	*have*

Collective Nouns: Singular or Plural Verbs?

A *collective noun* is a noun that stands for a group of people, places, or things. Following are some examples.

family	jury	flock	herd
orchestra	army	group	bunch

26

A collective noun may take either a singular or a plural verb, depending on what the speaker or writer means. When the speaker or writer is thinking of the group as a unit, the collective noun takes a singular verb.

The *family wants* to eat early. (it wants)

When the speaker or writer is thinking of the individual members of the group, the collective noun may take a plural verb.

The *family want* to eat at different times. (they want)

However, many writers and editors feel that this sounds awkward, and should be avoided entirely by rewriting the sentence.

The *members* of the family *want* to eat at different times.

Don't be fooled! Sometimes plural nouns find their way in between a collective noun and its verb.

A *bunch* /of grapes/*tastes* good after lunch.

A *flock*/of geese/*is flying* south.

If the bunch, the flock, or some other collective noun is acting as one unit, it still takes a singular verb, no matter how many other words come in between.

Compound Subjects

There are many ways to vary your sentences. Varying your sentences makes your writing more interesting. One way to vary your sentences is by using a *compound subject*. A *compound subject* is two or more subjects joined by a *coordinating* or *correlative conjunction*.

> *Lisa and I* went to the movies.
> *Rocky I* and *Rocky II* were playing on a double bill.

Other words can be part of a compound as well. Verbs, direct objects, and the objects of prepositional phrases can all be compounds. Direct objects and the objects of prepositional phrases are discussed on pages 42-44.

> **Compound verb:** I *hope* and *pray* to pass my Spanish test.

> **Compound direct object:** I like *hunting, fishing,* and *camping.*

> **Compound object of prepositional phrase:** I ran quickly through the *streets* and *byways.*

When you are connecting words within a sentence, make sure the words are in a similar form. Connect verbs with verbs, *-ing* words with *-ing* words, phrases with phrases, and so on.

> **Don't write:** She plans on *running laps* and *to work out* once school starts.

> **Write:** She plans on *running laps* and *working out* once school starts.

Or: She plans *to run laps* and *work out* once school starts.

Making Compound Subjects Agree with Verbs

Compound subjects joined by *and* usually take a plural verb.

Lisa and I always *go* to the movies together.

There are two exceptions. When the two words together form one item, use a singular verb.

Spaghetti and meatballs is my favorite dish.

My favorite *teammate* and *best friend is* Lisa.

Also, when the nouns are modified by *each* or *every*, use a singular verb.

Each movie and concert *is* being sponsored by our school.

Every student and teacher *has* an assignment to sell tickets.

When singular subjects are joined by *or*, use a singular verb.

Either the seaweed salad *or* the spider soup *is* free.

When one singular subject and one plural subject are joined by *or*, the verb agrees with the subject closest to it.

Either the Buffalo wings or the *spider soup is* free.

Either the spider soup or the *Buffalo wings are* free.

Chapter 10:
Predicates and Verbs
(What Happened?)

A *predicate* may include the most important word of a sentence. It can tell what the subject is or what the subject did. It also can tell what is being said about the subject. Look at the following sentences.

Johnetta is the fastest swimmer in our school.

The girl in the red suit is Johnetta.

Tired and happy, Johnetta finished her laps.

The *simple predicate* is the verb alone. The *complete predicate* includes all the adverbs, prepositions, nouns, conjunctions, and other words that go with the verb. In the sentences above, the complete predicate is underlined once, and the simple predicate is underlined twice.

Telling Time: Verb Tenses

The word *tense* refers to the form of the verb that tells you what time something took place. The form of a verb can tell you whether something happened in the *past,* the *present,* or the *future.*

Past	Present	Future
I *wanted* a new shirt.	I *want* a new shirt.	I *will want* a new shirt.
I *went* to the store.	I *go* to the store every day.	I *shall go* to the store tomorrow.

Principal Parts of Verbs

In order to form different verb tenses, you need to know the *principal parts* of a verb. Every verb has four principal parts:

► present infinitive
This form usually looks the same as the present tense, put with the word *to* in front. This is the form that you would look up in the dictionary.

(to) push   (to) wonder   (to) type

► present participle
The -*ing* form of a verb can be used either alone or with a form of *to be*.

(is) pushing (is) wondering (is) typing

► past
For regular verbs, this is formed by adding -*ed* or *d* to the present infinitive form.

pushed   wondered   typed

► past participle
For regular verbs, this is the same as the past form, but with some form of *to have*.

have pushed had wondered has typed

31

Choosing Verb Forms: Regular and Irregular Verbs

Every verb has different forms to talk about different times, or *tenses*. Most verbs follow a regular pattern for these forms. These are called *regular* verbs. Verbs with unusual or irregular patterns are called *irregular* verbs.

Unfortunately, because so many different languages have gone into creating the English language, there are many different forms of irregular verbs. This makes English a more interesting language—but it means that you will have to memorize a lot of irregular verbs!

Fortunately, irregular verbs do fall into certain patterns. Once you get a feel for each pattern, you will find it easier to remember the correct form of different verbs. Also, present participles are never irregular; they are always formed by adding *-ing.* Note the various patterns in the following groups of irregular verbs.

Present Infinitive	Present Participle	Past	Past Participle
burst	bursting	burst	burst
cost	costing	cost	cost
cut	cutting	cut	cut
hit	hitting	hit	hit
let	letting	let	let
put	putting	put	put
set	setting	set	set
wet	wetting	wet	wet

Present Infinitive	Present Participle	Past	Past Participle
hurt	hurting	hurt	hurt
bend	bending	bent	bent
build	building	built	built
lend	lending	lent	lent
send	sending	sent	sent
spend	spending	spent	spent
bring	bringing	brought	brought
buy	buying	bought	bought
catch	catching	caught	caught
fight	fighting	fought	fought
teach	teaching	taught	taught
think	thinking	thought	thought
bind	binding	bound	bound
find	finding	found	found
wind[1]	winding	wound	wound
bleed	bleeding	bled	bled
creep	creeping	crept	crept
feed	feeding	fed	fed
feel	feeling	felt	felt
keep	keeping	kept	kept
meet	meeting	met	met
sleep	sleeping	slept	slept
dream	dreaming	dreamt or dreamed	dreamt or dreamed
mean	meaning	meant	meant
read	reading	read	read
lead	leading	led	led
leave	leaving	left	left

[1]Don't confuse the past tense of *wind* with the present-tense form *wound*.
He *wound* the grandfather clock carefully.
Don't *wound* that rabbit!

The verb *wound* is a regular verb whose past is formed by adding *ed*.
The soldier was *wounded* in the war.

Present Infinitive	Present Participle	Past	Past Participle
dig	digging	dug	dug
spin	spinning	spun	spun
stick	sticking	stuck	stuck
sting	stinging	stung	stung
swing	swinging	swung	swung
hang	hanging	hung	hung
have	having	had	had
hear	hearing	heard	heard
hold	holding	held	held
lay	laying	laid	laid
lose	losing	lost	lost
make	making	made	made
pay	paying	paid	paid
say	saying	said	said
sell	selling	sold	sold
shoot	shooting	shot	shot
sit	sitting	sat	sat
stand	standing	stood	stood
tell	telling	told	told
win	winning	won	won
come	coming	came	come
run	running	ran	run
begin	beginning	began	begun
drink	drinking	drank	drunk
ring	ringing	rang	rung
shrink	shrinking	shrank	shrunk
sing	singing	sang	sung
sink	sinking	sank	sunk
stink	stinking	stank	stunk
swim	swimming	swam	swum

Present Infinitive	Present Participle	Past	Past Participle
be	being	was	been
beat	beating	beat	beaten
bite	biting	bit	bitten
blow	blowing	blew	blown
break	breaking	broke	broken
choose	choosing	chose	chosen
do	doing	did	done
draw	drawing	drew	drawn
drive	driving	drove	driven
eat	eating	ate	eaten
fall	falling	fell	fallen
fly	flying	flew	flown
forget	forgetting	forgot	forgotten
freeze	freezing	froze	frozen
get	getting	got	gotten
give	giving	gave	given
go	going	went	gone
grow	growing	grew	grown
hide	hiding	hid	hidden
know	knowing	knew	known
lie	lying	lay	lain
prove	proving	proved	proven
ride	riding	rode	ridden
rise	rising	rose	risen
see	seeing	saw	seen
shake	shaking	shook	shaken
show	showing	showed	shown
speak	speaking	spoke	spoken
steal	stealing	stole	stolen
take	taking	took	taken
tear	tearing	tore	torn
throw	throwing	threw	thrown

Present Infinitive	Present Participle	Past	Past Participle
wear	wearing	wore	worn
write	writing	wrote	written

Did you notice the patterns among the irregular verbs? For example, *wear, wearing, wore, worn* is similar to *tear, tearing, tore, torn.* These patterns can help you memorize irregular verbs. However, be careful. The verbs *bite* and *write* use the same pattern to form their past-participles, *bitten* and *written,* but are their past forms the same? Use the patterns to help you, but don't count on them too much.

Avoiding Some Common Mistakes: Gone versus Went; Saw versus Seen; Came versus Come

These verb forms are easy to mix up. However, once you get used to hearing them used in the way that is correct for Standard English, you will find it easy to use them in the right way. All you have to remember is which form is past and which is the past participle.

Past	Past Participle
went	(have) gone
saw	(had) seen
came	(has) come

The past form is used alone. The past-participle form is used with some form of the verb *to have.* To help you remember which is which, try memorizing these forms with the *have, had,* or *has* added to the past-participle form.

Another memorizing trick that will help you is to make up a sentence that uses each pair of words according to Standard English. If you remember the sentence, you can remember the way to use the words.

Here are three sentences that may work for you— or try making up your own.

I *went* to the circus because I *had* never *gone* before.

I *saw* things there I *had* never *seen* before.

As I *came* through the door, I said, "I *have come* home."

Choosing Between Active and Passive Voices

The *active voice* of a verb shows that a subject *does* the action and an object *receives* this action. (For more about objects, see Chapter 11 on page 42.)

Shagnasty *hit* the ball.

Marisol *snapped* her fingers.

Gonzo *whistled* a tune.

The *passive voice* of a verb shows that the subject of the sentence *receives* the action. The doer of the action is found within a prepositional phrase.

The ball *was hit* by Shagnasty.

Even though Shagnasty hit the ball, the word *ball* is the subject, because the verb *was hit* is in the passive voice.

To form the passive voice, take the base form of the verb and add some form of the verb *to be*.

Past: The ball *was hit* by Shagnasty.

Present: The ball *is hit* by Shagnasty.

Future: The ball *will be hit* by Shagnasty.

How do you know when to use the passive voice and when to use the active voice?

Many teachers and editors don't like the passive voice. They feel it makes writing less clear and strong. It's true that when used badly, the passive voice can be confusing, even funny.

Her fingers *were snapped* by Marisol.

Another problem with the passive voice is that it often gets the doer of the action "off the hook." Using the passive voice means that the doer of the action doesn't have to be mentioned at all.

All classes *have been canceled.*

All the money *will be collected.*

Our taxes *are being raised.*

Who canceled those classes? Who's collecting that money? Who is responsible for those higher taxes? Because the writer of the above sentence has used the passive voice, we don't know. Putting those sentences into the active voice makes the writer think about *who* is performing an action. Notice how much stronger these sentences sound when written in the active voice.

Our principal canceled all classes.

Ms. James will collect the money.

Governor Mercer is raising our taxes.

Sometimes, however, it is useful to use the passive voice. When you want the receiver of the action to be the focus of attention, you can use the passive. *Patrice* is the girl who *was hit* by the Frisbee.

Putting that sentence into the passive voice focuses the reader's attention on the word *Patrice,* rather than Frisbee. The passive voice is also useful when you don't know or don't want to stress the doer of the action. Chess *was invented* many years ago. The president *was elected* by a landslide.

A good rule to follow: When you find yourself using the passive voice, try changing the sentence into the active voice. If you think that improves the sentence, keep it active. If you think you've changed your meaning, change the sentence back to the passive.

The Subjunctive and Indicative Moods

Besides voices, verbs also have *moods.* Most sentences are in the *indicative* mood, which means simply that they indicate something. I *won* the chess tournament. Did you *go* to the finals?

But when something *might* happen, *would* happen, *could* happen, or *should* happen, it may be expressed in the *subjunctive* mood. If I *won* the chess tournament, I'd be very happy.

If you *had gone* to the finals, you would have seen me win.

The basic rule for the subjunctive is that it is used in instances *contrary to fact,* or when something didn't really happen. The most common use of it is with the word *were.*

> **Subjunctive:** If I *were* going to Mars, I'd take you there.
> **Simple past:** If I *was* wrong, I'm sorry.

In the first case, the speaker uses the subjunctive to express something that couldn't possibly be true: If I *were* going (but I'm not). In the second case, the speaker uses the simple past to express something that might or might not have been true. If I *was* wrong (I might or might not have been wrong).

Gerunds and Participles: Verbs Used as Nouns and Adjectives

A *gerund* is a verb form used as a noun. It looks like the present-participle form of a verb, but acts as a subject, direct object, or object of a preposition.

> **Verb:** Zelda *was going* to the store.
> **Gerund:** Zelda likes *going* to the store.

A *participle* is a verb form used as a noun or adjective. It can be formed from either the present or the past-participle form of the verb.

> **Verb:** Carmen *is inspiring* me to write a new song.

Noun: *Inspiring* an artist is a wonderful thing.
Adjective: I find this scene very *inspiring.*

A *perfect participle* is formed by combining the word *having* with the past-participle form of a verb. It is used as an adjective:

Having finished my work, I went home.
Having cheered for ten minutes, the crowd finally began to leave.

A Last Word on Infinitives

For many years, one of the rules of Standard English was: Never split an infinitive. That is, never put any word between *to* and the verb. To follow this rule, people found some pretty awkward ways of writing.

Split infinitive: *To* always *put* peanut butter on your food can be boring.
No split infinitive: Always *to put* peanut butter on your food can be boring.
Or: *To put* always peanut butter on your food can be boring.

This rule loosened up a little as the writers of grammar textbooks realized how difficult it was to follow. Now, it is generally considered acceptable to split an infinitive if it helps the sentence to make sense. However, be careful not to put too many words between the word *to* and the verb.

To always and with good intentions but still awkwardly *split* infinitives would be confusing!

Chapter 11:
Direct Objects and Indirect Objects
(Where Does the Action Go?)

Simple Objects

A word that receives the action of a transitive verb is called a *direct object*.

Pedro slammed the *door*.

He wanted a quick *snack*.

For more information on transitive verbs, see page 16.

An *indirect object* is the noun or pronoun that tells *to whom, to what, for whom,* or *for what* an action is done.

An indirect object appears only in combination with a direct object, never alone.

Hector gave *Harvey* the *ball*.

(*Ball* receives the action of the verb *gave* = direct object.

Harvey tells *to whom* Hector gave the ball = indirect object.)

42

Terry made *Jerry* a big *dinner.*

(*Dinner* receives the action of the verb *made* = direct object.

Jerry tells *for whom* Terry made the dinner = indirect object.)

To find the indirect object in a sentence, first look for the direct object. Ask *who* or *what* receives the action. Then look for the word that tells *to whom, to what, for whom,* or *for what* the action was done. That word is the indirect object. **Hint:** The indirect object comes between the verb and the direct object.

Mei Ling handed her friend a Frisbee.

> **Find direct object:** *Who* or *what* receives the action? The *Frisbee.*

> **Find indirect object:** *To whom* was the Frisbee handed? To *her friend.*

Mei Ling handed *her friend* a *Frisbee.*

Remember: If the word *to* or *for* is actually used in the sentence, the word that comes after it is not an indirect object. It's an object of the preposition.

> **Indirect object:** Mei Ling handed *her friend* a Frisbee.

> **Object of preposition:** Mei Ling handed a Frisbee to *her friend.*

Compound Objects

Both direct objects and indirect objects can be found in *compound* forms. That occurs when two or more nouns are joined by a conjunction. (See page 22 for conjunctions.) The conjunctions below are underlined twice.

Compound direct objects:

Pedro slammed the door and the window.

He wanted a quick snack and a rest.

Here are two examples of compound indirect objects.

Compound indirect objects:

Terry made Jerry, Murray, and Perry a big dinner.

Hector gave Harvey and Marvin a ball.

Chapter 12:
Predicate Nominatives and
Predicate Adjectives
(Pointing Back)

As we discussed earlier, linking verbs link the subject with the word or words that follow it. (For more information, see page 16.) Sometimes the words that come after linking verbs are nouns. These words identify the subject. They are called *predicate nominatives*. A *predicate nominative* is a noun or pronoun that comes after the verb and identifies the subject.

Ms. Shrink is a *teacher*.
She is a *specialist* in psychology.

Nominative means that the word *names* something, like a noun. The *predicate* is the part of the sentence that includes the verb. (For more information about predicates, see page 30.)

Sometimes the words that come after linking verbs are adjectives. These are called *predicate adjectives*. A *predicate adjective* is an adjective that comes after the verb and describes the subject.

Ms. Shrink seems *excited*.
She is *proud* of her new award.
Does she feel *happy*?

If a pronoun is used as a predicate nominative, it must agree with, or match, the subject. That means it must be in the subject case. (We'll talk more about case in the next chapter.)

Subject Case—for Predicate Nominatives

I
you
he, she, it
we
they

How do you know when a pronoun is a predicate nominative? The best way is to look for a linking verb. If a pronoun follows a linking verb and identifies the subject, it is probably a predicate nominative.

The new singer with the band <u>is I.</u>

The last singer <u>was she.</u>

The best audience for the group <u>is we.</u>

Chapter 13:
Pronouns and Their Antecedents
(Making a Case for It)

Choosing the Right Pronoun: I versus Me
and Other Problems

Some pronouns have different forms, depending on how they are used in the sentence. Most of the time, it's fairly easy to tell which form to use.

Right: *I* went to the store.
Wrong: *Me* went to the store.

These different forms are called *cases*. The *subject case* is used when the pronoun stands for someone or something that is performing the action. The *object case* is used when the pronoun stands for someone or something that the action is being directed to.

Subject-Case Pronouns	Object-Case Pronouns
I	me
you	you
he, she, it	him, her, it
we	us
they	them

Because you already know how to use these pronouns most of the time, what's the problem? Usually, the only difficulty comes up when there is more than one pronoun, or when the pronoun is paired with a noun.

> **Is it** *Bob and I* went to the store **or** *Bob and me* went to the store?

> **Is it** Lois gave the records to *Jay and me* **or** Lois gave the records to *Jay and I?*

The easiest way to choose the right pronoun in these cases is to cross out the noun and leave only the pronoun. Since you already know how to choose the right pronoun, you shouldn't have any trouble.

> ~~Bob and~~ me went to the store.
> *Me* went to the store? No!
> Bob and *I* went to the store.

> Lois gave the records to ~~Jay and~~ I.
> Lois gave the records to *I?* No!
> Lois gave the records to Jay and *me.*

When there are two pronouns, try each one separately.

> Her ~~and me~~ shared a soda.
> *Her* shared a soda? No!
> ~~Her and~~ me shared a soda.
> *Me* shared a soda? No!

Therefore, the correct choice must be:

Not *her*, but *she:* She shared a soda.
Not *me*, but *I:* I shared a soda.

She and *I* shared a soda.

Remember: Whenever a pronoun is used as a *direct object*, it is always used in the *object* case: *me, you, him, her, it, us,* or *them.*
Harvey asked *her* about the game.
She helped *him* with his pitching.

Likewise, a pronoun used as an *indirect object* is in the *object* case.

We gave *her* the news.
She showed *him* the paper.

Finally, a pronoun that is the *object* of a preposition should be in the *object* case:

Show the magazine to *us.*
Then give it to *them.*

Choosing the Right Pronoun: Who versus Whom

These days, most people don't bother very much about whether *who* or *whom* is correct when it comes to speaking. They usually just use *who* and forget about *whom.*

In writing, however, it's still important to use *who* only when it is the subject—the person or thing performing the action. In Standard English, you must use *whom* when it is the object—the person or thing receiving the action.

> **Subject:** *Who* is going to eat these brownies?
> **Object:** *Whom* did you ask to clean up the kitchen?

How can you tell when to use *who* and when to use *whom?* Don't worry. You already know when to use *he* and *him,* or *she* and *her.* (If you aren't sure, go back and read pages 47-49.) You can substitute the pronouns you already know how to use in the sentence. Just remember the *who formula:*

he	= who	him	= whom
she	= who	her	= whom

Choosing the Right Pronoun: Me versus Myself and Other Problems

The important thing to remember here is never to use *myself* when you can use *I* or *me.*

> **Wrong:** Boris and *myself* went to the movies.
> **Right:** Boris and *I* went to the movies.

> **Wrong:** Aunt Nell bought popcorn for Boris and *myself.*
> **Right:** Aunt Nell bought popcorn for Boris and *me.*

When do you use *myself* or other words that end in *-self* or *-selves?* These are always intensive or reflexive pronouns (see page 13.) They are used for emphasis or to refer back to another noun or pronoun.

Aunt Nell bought popcorn for *herself*.
She let Boris and me help *ourselves* to some.

And here's one more important thing to remember:

In Standard English, there are no such words as *theirself* or *theirselves*.
The correct word in Standard English is *themselves*.

Not: We were afraid the other team would hurt *theirself*.

But: We were afraid the other team would hurt *themselves*.

Likewise, there is no such word as *hisself* in Standard English. The word is *himself*.

Not: Seymour Snax helped *hisself* to the hot dogs.

But: Seymour Snax helped *himself* to the hot dogs.

Even though people may know what you mean if you use them, you will not be following the rules of Standard English. Remember, high schools, colleges, and most employers will expect you to follow these rules, particularly when you write.

Picking the Right Verb: Using Words
Like All, Some, and None

Some pronouns stand for nouns, persons, places, or things that are not definitely named. These are called *indefinite pronouns.*

Does *anyone* have a computer?
All of them are down today.

Notice how the first sentence uses a singular verb, *does have,* while the second uses a plural verb, *are.* Some indefinite pronouns are always used with singular verbs, some with plural verbs, and some with either kind of verb, depending on the meaning in the sentence. Here is a chart of the most common indefinite pronouns.

Indefinite Pronouns

Used with Singular Verb		Used with Plural Verb	Used with Singular or Plural Verbs
other	nothing	both	all
another	anything	few	any
everybody	something	many	more
anybody	everything	others	most
nobody	each	several	none
somebody	either		some
one	neither		enough
anyone	little		
someone	much		
everyone	no one		

You will just have to memorize the pronouns that are used with singular verbs and those that are used with plural verbs until you get a "feel" for them. How, then, can you tell whether to use a singular or a plural verb with the pronouns in the third part of the chart?

All of the cake *was* gone.
All of the guests *were* greedy.

The way to tell what kind of verb to use is to look at the words that come after *of*. If something singular—like *cake*—comes after *of*, use a singular verb. If something plural—like *guests*—comes after *of*, use a plural verb.

Let's see how this works. Suppose you were writing a sentence like the following:

run or runs

Most of the wolves _____ in packs.

You know that *most* sometimes takes a singular verb and sometimes takes a plural verb. (If you didn't remember this, you could have looked it up in the chart on page 52.) So you look at the words that come after *of—the wolves*. The word *wolves* is plural. So you know you should use a plural verb.

Most of the wolves *run* in packs.

Suppose, instead, you were writing this sentence:

is **or** are

Most of their time _____ spent hunting.

Again, you would look at the words that come after *of*. In this case, the words are *their time*. The word *time* is singular. So you should use a singular verb.

Most of their time *is* spent hunting.

Making Pronouns Clear: Using Antecedents

A pronoun's job in the sentence is to take the place of a noun. The noun that the pronoun stands for is called the *antecedent*. The antecedent can be in the same sentence as the pronoun.

Lila couldn't find the coat *she* bought.

The antecedent can also come in a different sentence.

Lila looked for her coat.
She sighed loudly.

A pronoun and its antecedent are supposed to match, or *agree*. In fact, there is a famous rule:

A pronoun must agree with its antecedent in *person, number,* and *gender.*

Agreeing in Person

Person is a term that describes the type of pronoun.

The person speaking is *first* person: I or we.
The person spoken to is *second* person: you.
The person spoken about is *third* person: he, she, or they.

This means that if the antecedent is in the third person, the pronoun should also be in the third person. In the following sentence, the pronoun and antecedent do not match in person.

If *people* want to buy new clothes, *you* have to earn money.

People is in the third person—the *people* are being spoken about—but *you* is in the second person, the one being spoken to. Since the two words are supposed to refer to the same thing, they have to match.

If *people* want to buy new clothes, *they* have to earn money.

Agreeing in Number

Number tells you whether the pronoun is singular or plural. *Singular* means there is only one; *plural* means there is more than one of whatever is being talked about.

Singular Pronouns	Plural Pronouns
I, me	we, us, our, ours
you, your, yours	you, your, yours
he, she, it,	they, them,
him, his, her, hers,	their, theirs
its	

In the following sentence, does the pronoun match its antecedent in number?

Every *boy* wants to look good for *their* first date.

The pronoun and antecedent do not match in that sentence. The antecedent, *boy*, is singular, but the pronoun, *their*, is plural. To make them match, you have to change either one or the other.

> **Singular:** Every *boy* wants to look good for *his* first date.
> **Plural:** All *boys* want to look good for *their* first date.

Agreeing in Gender

Gender tells you whether something is male, female, or neuter (neither male nor female, such as a chair, a book, or another object). It's usually easy to make pronouns and antecedents agree in gender. You would not be very likely to make the following mistake:

> Every *player* on the girl's basketball team went to *his* locker.

In this sentence, it is clear that *player* means "girl" and therefore requires a female pronoun. But what would you do in this sentence?

> his?
> Every coach spoke to _____ team.
> her?

Since a coach could be either a man or a woman, neither *his* nor *her* includes everybody.

56

You might be tempted to write the sentence like this:

Every coach spoke to *their* team.

But as we just saw, that won't work. *Coach* is singular; *their* is plural. The pronoun and antecedent must match in number as well as gender. Can you think of a solution? Actually, this is one of the most difficult problems in grammar, and many writers and editors still argue about how to solve it. Several years ago, many people believed that the word *he* or *his* could be used whenever both male and female were meant. These people would have argued that even if you were talking about both men and women coaches, you were correct in writing:

Every coach spoke to *his* team.

Nowadays, most people don't consider this acceptable. People today believe that it is not right to say just *his* when you are talking about both men and women. So these days, the sentence might be written:

Every coach spoke to *his or her* team.

Every coach spoke to *her or his* team.

Since it is awkward to keep repeating *her or his*, it is often easier to put the sentence in the plural:

All the coaches spoke to *their* teams.

Being Clear

Here is a sentence in which the pronouns and their antecedents match in person, number, and gender. But is the sentence clear?

> Leo and Sarah took the kittens to the vet, where they got special food to make their fur nice and shiny.

Whose fur was nice and shiny? Not Leo's and Sarah's! However, the reader might easily be confused about the antecedent of the word *their*. Does *their* refer back to Leo and Sarah or to the kittens?

If it is not clear which word a pronoun is referring to, either repeat the word or rewrite the sentence in some other way.

> Leo and Sarah took the kittens to the vet, where *the kittens* got special food to make their fur nice and shiny.

How would you rewrite the following unclear sentences?

> Jeannie told her mother that she had to return a phone call.
> (Who has to return the phone call? Jeannie or her mother?)

> A big cat should not be left alone with an angry dog or it could get hurt.
> (Who could get hurt? The cat or the dog?)

There are many ways you could rewrite those sentences. Following are a few choices.

Jeannie told her mother to return a phone call. (if the mother has to return the call)

Jeannie told her mother that she, Jeannie, had to return a phone call. (if Jeannie has to return the call)

A big cat should not be left alone with an angry dog or the cat could get hurt.

Does She Like Him Better Than Me or I?

Can you tell the difference between these two sentences?

She likes him better than me.
She likes him better than I.

The first sentence means that she likes him better than she likes me. The second means that she likes him better than I like him. The pronoun makes the difference. In the first sentence, it is in the object case. In the second, it is in the subject case.

If you think there is any doubt about your meaning, you might put in the extra words.

Object case: She likes him better than <u>she likes me.</u>

Subject case: She likes him better than <u>I like</u> him.

59

Chapter 14:
Modifiers: Adjectives and Adverbs
(Telling All About It)

A *modifier* is a word that tells more about another word. To *modify* something is to change it. A modifier modifies, or changes, the meaning of another word by telling more about it.

The two kinds of modifiers are *adjectives* and *adverbs*. *Adjectives* modify nouns (see page 18). *Adverbs* modify verbs, adjectives, other adverbs, and entire sentences. (For a review, see pages 19-20.)

Making Comparisons: Good, Better, Best, and Other Degrees

When two items are compared, adjectives are put in the *comparative degree*. This degree is usually formed by adding -*er*, or *more*, or *less*. The *superlative degree* is used for comparing three or more items. It is usually formed by adding -*est*, *most*, or *least*.

Most words of one syllable and some words of two or more syllables take -*er* and -*est* at the end. For remaining words of two or more syllables, add *more* and *most*.

For words ending in -*y* and -*ly*, sometimes you'll add -*er* and -*est*. Other times, you'll add *more* and *most*. If -*er* and -*est* are to be added, change the *y* to *i*.

happy	happier	happiest
friendly	friendlier	friendliest

When in doubt, you can't go wrong by adding *more* and *most*. However, never use *more* and *most* with words that already end in *-er* and *-est*.

Don't say: It was the *most happiest* time of my life.
Say: It was the *happiest* time of my life.

Don't say: The girls in our school are *more friendlier* than the boys.
Say: The girls in our school are *friendlier* than the boys.

These rules also apply to adverbs. Adjectives that follow these rules are known as *regular adjectives*. Adverbs that follow these rules are known as *regular adverbs*.

Some adjectives are irregular in their degrees of comparison. Only a few are irregular, but they include some of the most common words we use.

Irregular Adjectives

	Comparative	*Superlative*
good	better	best
bad	worse	worst
many	more	most
much	more	most
little	less	least
far (meaning distance)	farther	farthest

Likewise, some adverbs are irregular in their degrees of comparison, and these also include some of the most common words we use.

Irregular Adverbs

	Comparative	*Superlative*
well	better	best
badly	worse	worst
far (meaning extent)	further	furthest

Being Clear When Making Comparisons

> The team at Douglass School is better than Anthony School.

Does the writer really mean that the *team* is better than *Anthony School?* The writer probably meant to compare the team at Douglass to *the team* at Anthony. Without these extra words, the meaning isn't clear. This is an example of language that makes sense when you talk but can be hard to understand when you write. The writer would have been clearer by writing the following:

> The team at Douglass School is better than *the team at* Anthony School.

> **Don't write:** The players at Douglass are better than Anthony.

> **Write:** The players at Douglass are better than *those at* Anthony.

62

Double Negatives

Another kind of adverb is the *negative* adverb. These also modify verbs by answering the question *how, when,* or *to what extent.*

I *can't* see. (*How* can you see? You *cannot.*)
I will *never* come. (*When* will you come? Never!)
I can *hardly* believe it. (*To what extent* can you believe it? Hardly!)

Negative Adverbs

hardly	never	not	nowhere
scarcely	barely	n't (used as part of contraction)	

Other Negative Words

no	no one	none
nothing	nobody	

In Standard English, it is not considered correct to use two negative words in close relationship with each other.

Double negative: I *can't hardly* believe it.
Standard English: I *can hardly* believe it.

Double negative: You *don't never* listen.
Standard English: You *don't ever* listen
or You *never* listen.
To avoid double negatives, just change one of the negative words into a positive word, or drop one of the negative words.

Double negative: I *don't* see *nothing* else to do.
Standard English: I *don't* see *anything* else to do **or** I see *nothing* else to do.

Choosing Between Adverbs and Adjectives: Good versus Well and Other Problems

Sometimes it's difficult to know when to use an adjective and when to use an adverb. This is true for many reasons. Not all words ending in *-ly* are adverbs and not all adverbs end in *-ly*, so it may be confusing to choose by "sound." Some words can be used as either adverbs or adjectives, such as *well, deep,* and *high.* Also, it's sometimes unclear whether a verb is a linking verb or an action verb. This can make it hard to know whether the verb requires an adjective or an adverb.

The good news is that once you understand the basic principles behind choosing between adjectives and adverbs, it's not so hard to get them right. Let's break the problem down into separate parts so that it's easier to understand.

Good versus Well, Bad versus Badly

These four words are probably the trickiest of all. That's because *bad* is almost always an adjective.

> **Adjective with linking verb:** She *felt* bad.
> (She felt sorry, sick, or sad.)
> **Adjective with noun:** The *bad* girl felt happy.
> (*Bad* answers the question *which girl.*)

Likewise, *good* can only be used as an adjective.

Adjective with linking verb: She felt *good.*
(She felt happy.)

Adjective with noun: The *good* girl felt happy.
(*Good* answers the question *which girl.*)

Badly can only be used as an adverb. *Well,* on the other hand, can be used as either an adverb or an adjective.

Adjective with linking verb:
I feel *good.*
(I feel happy.)
I feel *well.*
(I feel in good health.)
I feel *bad.*
(I feel sorry, sick, or sad.)

Adverb with action verb:
I work *well* in the mornings.
(I work in a good way.)
I work *badly* in the evenings.
(I work in a bad way.)

The only way to choose correctly among these words is to memorize what each of them means. Try using these "memorizer" sentences to help you keep the meanings of good, well, bad, and badly straight in your mind.

Adjective:	That was a *good* song,
Adverb:	and you sang it *well.*
Adjective:	That was a *bad* song,
Adverb:	and you sang it *badly.*
Adjective:	Don't you feel *well?*

Other Confusing Pairs

Again, the best way to sort these pairs out is to memorize short sentences in which they are used correctly according to the rules of Standard English. You can use the sample sentences below, or you can write your own. Remembering the word in a sentence will help you get used to the ''sound'' or the ''feel'' of Standard English.

Adjective:	This chain is *real* gold.
Adverb:	It is *really* shiny.
Adjective:	I am *sure.*
Adverb:	I am *surely* in love.
Adjective:	That song was *awful.*
Adverb:	It was *awfully* loud.
Adjective:	That question was *easy,*
Adverb:	and I answered it *easily.*

Words That Can Be Either Adjectives or Adverbs

Many words can be either adjectives or adverbs, depending on how they are used. Following are some ''memorizer'' sentences that show the different ways each word can be used.

Adverb:	We started *early*
Adjective:	for the *early* show.
Adverb:	The cowboy rode *fast*
Adjective:	on a *fast* horse.

Adverb:	We started *late*
Adjective:	for the *late* show.
Adverb:	We sailed *slow* (**or** *slowly*)
Adjective:	on a *slow* boat.
Adverbs:	We looked *high* and *low,*
Adjectives:	on the *high* shelf and in the *low* cupboard.
Adverb:	We didn't look *long*
Adjective:	for the *long* spoon.
Adverb:	She stood *near*
Adjective:	the sail on the *near* side.

Sometimes there are two forms of an adverb, one with *-ly* and one without.

He drove *slow.* He drove *slowly.*

Often, the *-ly* form has a slightly different meaning from the other form.

Here the diver has to swim *deep.*
He felt its beauty *deeply.*

The judge banged her gavel *hard.*
There was *hardly* enough time for the trial.

                   adjective   **adverb**
We went to the *late* show because *lately* we
                            adverb
have been staying out *late.*

Chapter 15:
Phrases and Clauses
(Two Groups You Should Know)

What Is A Phrase?

A *phrase* is a group of related words that does not have a subject or a predicate. In other words, it does not express a complete thought. Phrases include *verb phrases, adjective phrases, adverb phrases,* and *participial phrases.*

Verb phrase: I *will be going* to the moon.

Adjective phrase: The man *in the helmet* will take me.

Adverb phrase: Together we will fly *deep into space.*

Participial phrase: The first teenager *landing on the moon* will be I.

An *adjective phrase* is two or more words that work together to modify a noun or pronoun.

The plane *in the hangar* was ready to leave.

An *adverb phrase* is two or more words that work together to modify a verb, an adjective, or another adverb.

The plane flew quickly *into the sky.*

What Is a Clause?

A *clause* is a group of words having a subject and a predicate. It may or may not express a complete thought. Clauses that express complete thoughts can stand alone as sentences, but more often, the word *clause* is used to refer to only part of a sentence.

Noun Clauses

A *noun clause* is a group of words that has a subject and a predicate and functions as a noun. A noun clause can take the place of a subject, a predicate nominative, an indirect object, a direct object, or the object of a preposition.

> **Subject:** *Whoever ate the ice cream* must buy us all some more!
>
> **Indirect object:** Give *whoever ate the ice cream* some more money.
>
> **Direct object:** Don't scold *whoever ate the ice cream.*
>
> **Object of a preposition:** What was the favorite flavor of *whoever ate the ice cream?*
>
> **Predicate nominative:** The problem is *that whoever ate the ice cream* won't confess!

> Here are some words that can come at the beginning of a noun clause: *who, whoever, whom, whomever, whose, whosoever, which, whichever, what, whatever, whether, when, where, why, how, if,* and *that.*

Adjective Clauses

Another kind of dependent clause is called an *adjective clause*. This type of clause modifies a noun or a pronoun by telling *what kind* or *which one*. An adjective clause usually begins with a *relative pronoun*. Relative pronouns relate the clause to the noun or pronoun.

Relative Pronouns
that
which
who, whom, whose
whoever, whomever

The movie *that we saw* was fantastic!
(tells which movie)
The story, *which was a real thriller*, kept me on the edge of my seat.
(tells what kind of movie)
The heroine was looking for the man *who killed her brother*.

A famous movie star, *whose name I can't remember*, played the killer.

Adverb Clauses

An *adverb clause* is a group of words with a subject and a predicate that takes the place of an adverb. Like an adverb, it tells *how, where, why, when, to what extent*, and *how much*.

An adverb clause begins with a *subordinating conjunction*. (For more about the different types of conjunctions, see page 22.)

70

Subordinating Conjunctions

after	before	until
although	if	when
as	since	whenever
as if	so that	where
as much as	than	wherever
as long as	though	whether
as soon as	unless	while
as though		
because		

Adverb clause telling how: She stood *so that she could see the screen.*

Adverb clause telling when: She had arrived *as soon as the show began.*

Adverb clause telling why: *Because she enjoyed the music,* she wanted to be on time.

Adverb clause telling where: *Wherever she moved,* though, she couldn't see.

Adverb clause telling to what extent: She was more frustrated *than she had ever been before.*

Adverb clause telling how much: Then she found a good spot and could see *as much as she wanted to.*

Dependent and Independent Clauses

A *clause* is any group of words that has a subject and a predicate. (See pages 24-30.) Some clauses are sentences; some are not. A clause that can stand alone is called an *independent clause.*

Our rocket is leaving tomorrow.

71

A clause that cannot stand alone is called a *dependent clause.*

Although we are short of fuel,

A dependent clause must be combined with one or more independent clauses to make a complete sentence.

Although we are short of fuel, our rocket is leaving tomorrow.

In the above sentence, the dependent clause is underlined twice; the independent clause is underlined once.

Part III: SENTENCES
(Putting the Pieces Together)

Chapter 16:
Types of Sentences (. ? !)

What Is a Sentence?

A sentence is a group of words with a subject and a predicate that expresses a complete thought. It must begin with a capital letter and end with some form of end punctuation: a period, a question mark, or an exclamation point. Some sentences can make up part of compound or complex sentences; these sentences "within sentences" can be punctuated differently. Nevertheless, there must be some form of *end* punctuation!

Types of Sentences

Declarative Sentences. A sentence that makes a simple declaration, or statement, is called a *declarative sentence.* It ends with a period. Most sentences are declarative sentences.

> I am going fishing.
> The president knows what to do.
> You should dye your hair green.

Interrogative Sentences. A sentence that interrogates, or asks a question, is known as an *interrogative sentence.* An interrogative sentence is also known as a *question.*

You can make an interrogative sentence simply by putting a question mark at the end of a declarative sentence.

> I am going fishing?
> The president knows what to do?
> You should dye your hair green?

Also, you can reverse the order of some words, or add a few extra words, in order to show that you are asking a question.

> Am I going fishing?
> Does the president know what to do?
> Should you dye your hair green?

Note: Can you tell the slight difference in shades of meaning that takes place when you change the word order?

Exclamatory Sentences. As you might expect, exclamatory sentences express strong feeling and end in exclamation points. Again, these may be identical to interrogative or declarative sentences, except for the punctuation changes.

> I am going fishing!
> The president knows what to do!
> You should dye your hair green!

Note: Again, changing even something so tiny as a punctuation mark changes the meaning of a sentence. Be aware of these changes so that you can use them in your writing.

Sentence Structure

Simple Sentences

The simplest form of a sentence is called, not surprisingly, a *simple sentence.* In a simple sentence, there is only one independent clause. A simple sentence may be quite long but will still contain only one independent clause. In the examples below, the subjects are underlined once, and the simple predicates are underlined twice.

I am tired.

I am going to Paris, France, and Mexico City, Mexico.

As you have learned, sentences may have compound subjects, compound predicates, compound direct objects, and compounds of just about every other sentence part. No matter which compounds a sentence has, however, it is still a simple sentence if it has only one independent clause.

Jose and Paul skipped and jumped over the rocky path.
The two boys and their friends finished their walk, found a restaurant, and went inside.

Compound Sentences

A *compound sentence* shows a close connection between two equally important and related ideas.

> The test was too hard and it lasted too long.
>
> The game was great and the party afterward was even better.

In the sentences above, the parts of the compound sentence are joined by the word *and* without a comma. Since the clauses are so short, no comma is necessary. For longer clauses connected by a coordinating conjunction, use a comma before the conjunction. You should also use a comma to avoid confusion.

> I wanted to run for office myself, but later I decided to vote for Honest Ollie.
>
> I voted for Ollie, and Mark did too.

Parts of a compound sentence may also be linked with a semicolon (;).

> I saw Daphne at the dance; it was hard to find her.
> The room was dark; Rudolph had trouble seeing.

A colon (:) is sometimes used when the second part of a compound sentence explains the first.

> One fact remained clear: We were going to have to change our plans.

Complex Sentences

A *complex sentence* consists of one independent clause and at least one dependent clause.

A dependent clause often begins with a word known as a *subordinating conjunction*. To subordinate something means to make it less important or less powerful. A subordinating conjunction shows that the dependent clause is less "powerful" than the independent clause because it cannot stand alone.

Because I wanted ice cream,

Although I never saw her before,

Unless you stop stuffing your face,

None of these clauses makes sense without the rest of the sentence.

I told them to hurry because I wanted ice cream.

Although I never saw her before, Mia helped as much as anyone else.

Unless you stop stuffing your face, you will never lose weight.

Usually, if a dependent clause begins a sentence, you should use a comma after it. In most cases, don't use a comma before a dependent clause that ends a sentence.

After the party was over, we had to clean up.

We had to clean up after the party was over.

Words That Often Start Dependent Clauses

Prepositions		Adverbs	Subordinating Conjunctions	
after	while	when	if	unless
before	until	how	although	because
		where	whereas	though
		why		

Remember: Don't confuse a dependent clause that begins with a preposition with a prepositional phrase. A clause has a subject and a verb; a prepositional phrase has only a preposition and its object.

    Clause: After the party was over,

    Phrase: After the party,

Chapter 17:
Fragments and Run-on Sentences
(Bits and Pieces)

Avoiding Fragments

A *sentence fragment* is a group of words that does not form a complete thought and so is not a sentence. One single word can form a sentence; many words strung together may form a fragment. The difference is not in how long the words go on, but in whether they form a complete thought.

Sentence: Stop!
Fragment: After the movie, which was very interesting.

The first sentence is complete. We understand that the speaker or writer wants someone to stop. The subject is understood to be "you." The fragment, on the other hand, is not complete. We want to ask, *"What happened* after the movie, which was very interesting?"

Here again, patterns that may work in speaking don't work in writing. The fragment above might have made more sense in conversation. On paper, out of context, it leaves the reader frustrated and puzzled. Following are two ways to spot fragments so that you can make them into full sentences.

Ask yourself if there is a subject and a verb. If there is not, you have a fragment. (In a sentence like "Stop!" the subject, "you," is understood. In most other sentences, the subject is named explicitly.)

Even if there is a subject and a verb, the group of words might be a dependent clause. If it begins with one of the words in the chart on page 78, it is probably a dependent clause and therefore a fragment if used alone.

Avoiding Run-on Sentences

Make sure that the parts of your command sentence are actually related. Run-on sentences are hard to understand, because they give the reader more than one complete thought to think about.

A *run-on sentence* combines two or more sentences into one, with a misplaced comma or no punctuation at all. It can usually be corrected with a period, a semicolon, or a comma and a coordinating conjunction (for example, *and* or *but).*

> **Run-on sentence:** I gave the records to Michelle, she likes that kind of music.
>
> **Compound and simple sentences:** I gave the records to Michelle. She likes that kind of music. **Or** I gave the records to Michelle; she likes that kind of music.

Sentences that are overly long are also hard to follow, even if they are grammatically correct. Putting in periods and other punctuation is like pausing and stressing words when you speak. It lets your audience know what you mean.

Part IV: COMMON MISTAKES (...And How To Avoid Them)

As we have seen, English can be a tricky language! Even people who have been studying grammar for years find themselves making mistakes.

To recognize and correct your own mistakes, you will need to know the rules of Standard English. They can help you with your writing in high school, at college, or on the job. This chapter will help you with some of the trickiest choices in English.

Chapter 18:
Confusing and Dangling Modifiers
(Making It Clear)

Confusing Phrases

In English, where you place a phrase can have a lot to do with the meaning of a sentence. For example, look at the difference between these two sentences.

Do you have a lot of work for me to do?
Do you have a lot of work to do for me?

Changing the position of just four little words changes the meaning of the whole sentence.

Participial phrases are especially tricky. They usually modify the word they come right after in the sentence.

The woman *wearing the blue hat* ordered coffee.

So be careful: If you write this sentence out of order, it may mean something quite different!

The woman ordered coffee wearing a blue hat.

Unless the woman wants a hat on her coffee, the sentence is not clear.

How would you correct the following sentences?

Cooked with bacon, I will eat liver, but not served plain.

Linda found the machine reaching high onto the shelf.

The first sentence sounds as though the writer is cooked with bacon! Moving the phrase helps make the sentence clear.

I will eat liver cooked with bacon, but not served plain.

The phrase now comes after the word it describes.

Unless Linda's machine is reaching high onto the shelf, the second sentence is also unclear. It might be awkward to put the phrase *reaching high onto the shelf* right after *Linda,* but how about putting it before?

Reaching high onto the shelf, Linda found the machine.

Now there is no chance for confusion.

Dangling Modifiers

Sometimes, writers will use an *-ing* word without being clear about what the word is supposed to describe.

Walking down the street, the church was on my left.

Is the church walking down the street? If not, who is? The word *walking* is called a *dangling modifier* because, although it is supposed to modify a word, it just "dangles," or hangs, in the sentence with nothing to modify. Be sure that *-ing* words in a sentence clearly describe the noun or pronoun they belong with in the sentence.

Walking down the street, *I* saw the church on my left.
The church was on my left *as I was* walking down the street.

83

Chapter 19:
Who versus Which versus That
(Making A Choice)

These words can be confusing because they all play similar roles in a sentence. However, each is slightly different. *Who* refers to people only. *That* refers to people, animals, or things. *Which* refers to animals or things only.

That clears up the question of *who* versus *which* and *that*. But how do you know when to use *which* and when to use *that?*

Here is a fairly simple formula that will keep you out of trouble: *That* is used for clauses that define or identify the subject. *Which* is used for clauses that may give additional information, but are not needed to identify the subject.

The book *that I wanted* is on your desk.

Here, the clause *that I wanted* is needed to answer the question *which book*. Without the clause, we would not be able to identify the subject.

The book, *which I wanted,* is on your desk.

In the second sentence, the clause gives additional information about the book, but is more an extra remark than necessary information. The clause does not identify *which book,* but only tells more about the book. If you are using *which,* make sure to put a comma before the *which* and after the end of the clause. If you are using *that,* don't use a comma.

Chapter 20:
Them versus These versus Those
(Getting It Right)

The confusion here is caused by the fact that some words can double as both pronouns and adjectives. *Those* and *these* can either stand alone as pronouns or come before nouns as adjectives.

Pronoun: *Those* are the tickets I want.

Adjective: *These* tickets are for the wrong concert.

Them, however, is only a pronoun, never an adjective. So it is never correct in Standard English to use *them* just before a noun.

Not Standard English: I want *them* tickets.
Standard English: I want *those* tickets.

Also, since *them* is an object-case pronoun, it can't be used as a subject.

Not Standard English: *Them* are for the wrong concert.
Standard English: *These* are for the wrong concert.

It is also not Standard English to use expressions such as *this here* or *that there*.

Chapter 21:
Tricky Verbs
(Choosing the Right One)

Many verbs sound very similar but actually have different meanings. There is a more complete list of tricky and easily confused words starting on page 89. However, following are some of the most often confused.

Sit versus Set

Sit means to take a seat. *Set* means to place something or to put something down.

> All of the parents should *sit* here.
> We will *set* the chairs up in neat rows.

Remember that *sit* is something the subject does himself or herself; *set* is something the subject does to another object.

> I won't *sit* down until you *set* down that book.

Lay versus Lie

Just like *sit* and *set,* *lay* and *lie* have two different meanings. *Lay* means to put or place. *Lie* means to rest or recline.

Like *set*, *lay* tells what the subject does to an object. Like *sit*, *lie* is something the subject does himself or herself.

Would you like to *lie* down?
Lay that plate on the table, please.

The two verbs have different past and participle forms.

lay	laying	laid	laid
lie	lying	lay	lain

Forms of lie: I am *lying* down after dinner.
Yesterday I *lay* down after lunch.
Often I *have lain* down on the couch.

Forms of lay: I like *laying* the plates close to the edge of the table.
I *laid* that book down and now I can't find it.
Have you *laid* out the place mats yet?

Finally, don't confuse the *lie* that means "to lie down" with the *lie* that means "not to tell the truth."

To lie down:	lie	lying	lay	lain
Not to tell the truth:	lie	lying	lied	lied

I don't like to *lie*.
I am not *lying* now.
Once, long ago, I *lied* to my best friend.
Whenever I *have lied,* I have regretted it.

Raise versus Rise

Raise means to move something upward. *Rise* means to go upward.

So again, *rise* is something the subject does itself. *Raise* is something the subject does to something else.

The balloon *rises* slowly into the air.
Will you *raise* that ladder so I can pass?

Be careful about the past and participle forms of these two words.

raise	raising	raised	raised
rise	rising	rose	risen

Raise: We're *raising* the roof!
We *raised* a lot of money last week at our dance.
Have you *raised* the fee we pay the band?

Rise: I'm *rising* early in the morning.
Yesterday I *rose* at seven o'clock.
The sun *had* already *risen* when I got up.

Chapter 22:
Words That Are Often Confused
(Tricky Mix-Ups)

a: Use *a* before words that start with a consonant sound: *a* book, *a* dog, *a* union, *a* youth.

an: Use *an* before words that start with a vowel sound: *an* apple, *an* honor.

accept: to take or to receive
except: but

Everyone *except* Lou got to *accept* a medal.

advice: an opinion
advise: to give advice

I *advise* you to take his *advice*.

affect: to have an influence on
effect: a result

I was *affected* by that sad music.
The music had a big *effect* on me.

all right: OK
alright: **not** a word in Standard English

already: by this time, previously
all ready: prepared, all set

> It was *already* three o'clock by the
> time I was *all ready* to go.

anywhere: anyplace
anywheres: **not** a word in Standard English

beside: next to
besides: in addition to

> *Besides* all my other troubles, I had to
> sit *beside* my English teacher at the rally.

breathe: to draw air into the lungs
breath: the air you draw into your lungs

> It was so stuffy, I couldn't *breathe*.
> When I got outside, I took a deep *breath*.

bring: to come here with something
take: to go there with something

> *Bring* me some good news from the
> meeting.
> *Take* these refreshments to the meeting.

choose: the present tense, meaning "to select"
         or "to pick out"
chose: the past tense, "to select" or "to pick out "

> Today I *choose* the chocolate cake.
> Yesterday I *chose* the carrot cake.

clothes: what you wear
cloths: pieces of material or fabric

Pat always wears great *clothes*.
At the fabric store, we saw many beautiful
cloths for covering tables.

conscience: ideas and feelings about right
             and wrong
conscious: being awake or aware

My *conscience* bothered me about that lie.
I was *conscious* that you were in the room.

human: being a person or like a person
humane: merciful

Laughter is a *human* activity; animals
don't laugh.
It is not *humane* to punish people
without a reason.

idea: a thought or opinion
ideal: something that is perfect or a perfect example

Pete had a good *idea* yesterday.
I admire Pete very much; he is my *ideal*.

in: used to show where something is
into: used to show movement from one place
      to another

Jorge was *in* the car. I got *into* the car
with him.

later: the comparative form of *late*
latter: the second of two

> It's *later* than you think!
> If you can see the ladder and the can of paint, bring me the *latter*, which would be the can of paint.

learn: to receive instruction
teach: to give instruction

> I will *learn* how to drive if you *teach* me.
> I don't know how to drive, so I must *learn*.
> Since you do know how to drive, you can *teach* me.

let: to give permission or to allow
leave: to go away

You can use either word with *alone*. In most other confusing situations, use *let*.

> *Let* me alone!   *Leave* me alone!
> *Let* go of that doorknob.
> *Let* the door stay closed.

loose: not tight, not close together
lose: to suffer a loss

> She tied the rope in a *loose* knot.
> She didn't want the horse to get *loose*.
> She couldn't afford to *lose* the horse.

nowhere: no place
nowheres: **not** a word in Standard English

quit: to stop
quiet: silent or silence
quite: very

> I *quit* my job because it was too *quiet* there.
> The *quiet* made me *quite* nervous!

than: in comparison with
then: at that time

> *Then* he said he was older *than* his brother.

to: toward
two: the number after *one*
too: also

> I went *to* *two* stores, and to the bakery, *too.*

Part V: PUNCTUATION AND CAPITALIZATION
(Making Your Mark)

Chapter 23:
Capital Letters
(The Big Ones)

Capitalize the beginning of every sentence.

I bought a model airplane yesterday.
How do you read those directions?
This is much too hard!
Stop! Have a little patience!

Capitalize all names of people, and the word *I*.

Sarah Bill Mei Ling Pablo Dracula
the Jones family   Hirsch's   Angie Robles

Capitalize all names of particular places: cities, states, countries, rivers, oceans, streets, parks, lakes, and so forth.

Mississippi   Shoreview Drive
Akron, Ohio   Lake Ontario   Red River
Lookout Park

Capitalize the names of the days of the week, the months, and holidays. Do not capitalize ''little'' words in holidays. Do not capitalize the four seasons.

Capitalize: Monday, Wednesday
January, April,
Christmas, Hanukkah,
Ramadan

Don't Capitalize: winter, summer,
spring, fall, autumn

And remember: the Fourth of July

Capitalize the names of religions, nationalities, languages, and the adjectives that are made from these words.

Jewish, Catholic, Protestant, Christian, Moslem, French, Afro-American, English, Hispanic, Puerto Rican, Arab-American

Capitalize ranks or titles only when they are used with a person's name.

Doctor Ellen Glass, Judge Felipe Lopez
But: The judge said he was starting the trial.

Capitalize words that show family relationships only when they are used with a person's name.

Aunt Molly Jackson, Cousin Jess
But: My aunt and my cousin came to dinner.

If you are using the family word instead of the person's name, then capitalize it.

Well, Dad, how are you tonight?

My dad and I go fishing every summer.

Capitalize the name of the Deity except when refering to a pagan god (as in the gods of mythology). Capitalize the name of sacred documents.

God, Allah, Jesus, Jehovah, the Torah, the Koran, the Bible

Capitalize the names of schools, companies, buildings, government departments, and organizations, but do not ordinarily capitalize such "little words" as *a, an, the, of,* and *on.*

Hilldale High School, Pacific Bell Telephone, the Chrysler Building, the State Department, the Department of Commerce, the National Organization for Women, the Boy Scouts

Capitalize names of historical periods and events.

World War I, the Renaissance, the Civil War, the Roaring Twenties

Capitalize the names of planets. Do not capitalize *sun, moon,* or *earth* except when *earth* is used as the name of the planet.

Mars, Venus, Jupiter, Saturn
In between Venus and Mars is Earth.
The worm burrowed deep into the earth.

Capitalize *east, west, north,* and *south* when they refer to a particular section of the country or the world. Do not capitalize them when they are showing direction.

The East has many big cities.
Turn east on the highway.
She has an Eastern accent.

Capitalize all the main words in a title, including the first and last words. Do not capitalize "little" words such as *a, an, of, the,* and *on* unless they are the first or last words.

"The Raven," "Casey at the Bat,"
A Tale of Two Cities, West Side Story,
The Wizard of Oz

Do not capitalize school subjects unless they are the names of nationalities or languages, or unless you are writing the title of a course.

Capitalize: French, English, Spanish,
American history, English literature
Biology 101

Do not capitalize: science, math, calculus,
literature, geography, civics

Chapter 24:
Periods and Commas
(Stop...or Pause)

Using Periods

Most sentences end in *periods.* Use a period at the end of any sentence that does not ask a question or express strong feelings.

I am going to the store now.

You should also use a period after abbreviations. The period shows that some letters have been left out. Initials—the first letters of names—are abbreviations that require periods.

lb., St., Dr., Mr., Ms., U.S.A., J.R. Ewing, Dr. L. Jean Santiago

Some abbreviations do not require periods. These include the postal abbreviations for states and some names of organizations.

MN, ND, NY, NATO, OAS, UN

There are no real rules for which abbreviations require periods and which do not. You simply have to memorize them. Generally, if you make sure to use periods after initials and abbreviated titles—*Dr., Mr., Ms.,* and so forth—you will be on firm ground.

Using Commas

The *comma* is used to separate words or phrases in a series. Some people prefer putting a comma before the word *and* or *or* (called the *serial comma*); some people leave it out. The choice is usually up to you.

Washington, Adams, and Jefferson were our first three presidents.
Blood, Sweat and Tears is one of my favorite rock groups.
I ordered the pizza, cleaned up the living room, and got dressed for the party.

If there are two or more adjectives of equal importance in a phrase, a comma must be used to separate them.

A close, exciting election took place.

However, sometimes a comma is not used between adjectives.

I wore dark blue wool slacks to the party.

If you can put *and* between the adjectives or change their order around, they need to be separated by a comma.

I wore dark and blue and wool slacks? No! No comma.
A close and exciting election took place.
An exciting and close election took place.
Yes. Comma is needed.

A comma is usually needed before the coordinating conjunction—*and, but, or, nor, for, so,* or *yet*—connecting two independent clauses to make a compound sentence. However, if the clauses are very short, you may not need a comma. For more information, see page 76.

> I walked the dog and Maria fed the cat.
> I wanted to take the dog to the vet, but Maria told me to wait for Mother.

You should use a comma after certain kinds of words, phrases, and clauses that begin sentences.

Use Commas after Exclamations

If a sentence begins with *oh, yes, no, well, hey, say,* or a similar expression, use a comma.

> Hey, I wasn't finished yet.
> Yes, I do mind.

Use Commas after Prepositional Phrases

If a sentence begins with a long prepositional phrase, use a comma after the phrase.

> In the first place, I was still reading it.
> In my opinion, that's very rude.

Use Commas after Some Adverbs

Some adverbs are used to begin sentences. These words comment on the entire sentence. You should almost always use a comma after such adverbs. (For more information about these adverbs, see page 20.)

Fortunately, we have more than one
paper.
Unfortunately, I can't find the second one.

Sometimes, however, you don't need to use a
comma after an adverb that begins a sentence.

Apparently you think I have nothing better
to do.
Suddenly the new nation had its first
president.

If you are unsure, it's probably better to put the
comma in.

Use Commas after Adverb Clauses
When an adverb clause begins a sentence, you
should put a comma after it.

After Jo comes back, let's read the paper
together.

Use Commas after Participial Phrases
Likewise, when a participial phrase begins a
sentence, it usually needs a comma.

Reading the paper together, we discovered
some exciting news.

However, don't use a comma if the participial phrase
is the subject of the sentence.

Reading the paper together is a pleasant
way to spend time.

Commas are also needed to separate a person's name from the rest of the sentence if the person is being spoken to directly.

> Doctor, is there enough time for the operation?

> Please give this note to the doctor, Aunt Jill.

Use Commas in Addresses

A comma goes between each part of the address—after the name, the street, and the city. If the address comes in the middle of a sentence, a comma goes after the state as well.

> Send the package to Ms. Lillian Marquez, 425 W. 25th St., New York, New York 10026.

> I saw that the letter was addressed to New York, New York, in a neat, careful handwriting.

But don't use commas in the address on the front of an envelope, except between city and state.

> Ms. Lillian Marquez
> 425 W. 25th St.
> New York, NY 10026

Use Commas in Dates

Use a comma between the day and the year when writing a date. If the date comes in the middle or at the beginning of a sentence, put a comma after the year.

January 23, 1955   July 4, 1776
On July 4, 1776, the Declaration of
Independence was signed.

Use Commas to Set Off Interrupters
Use a comma to set off words that interrupt a sentence.

Our team, in my opinion, is the best in the state.
You see, we practice hard every day.
For example, we practiced last Sunday.
Sunday practice went very well, by the way.

Use Commas to Separate Nonessential Information
Use a comma to separate information that is not essential.

The two cats, restless and hungry, went into the kitchen.
They were looking for the cans of cat food, which had not yet been opened.

Nonessential information is information that can be left out and still allow the sentence to make sense.

Use Commas to Avoid Confusion
The following sentence illustrates the use of a comma to avoid confusion.

Several hours before, we fed the cats.

Chapter 25:
The Apostrophe
(What's Missing...Who Owns It?)

How to Use an Apostrophe

An *apostrophe* has two different uses. Earlier, we saw it used to show possession. See page 12.

However, it can stand for some letters that have been left out.

> *It is* time to start dancing!
>
> *It's* time to start dancing.

Words that have been shortened with an apostrophe are called *contractions*. Some contractions are *he's, she's, I'm, can't,* and *it's.*

How do you know when to use an apostrophe and when not to use one?

It's simple. You never use an apostrophe with one of the following *personal possessive pronouns*, because they *already* show possession. They don't need an apostrophe.

Personal Possessive Pronouns	
my, mine	our, ours
your, yours	your, yours
his, her, hers, its	their, theirs

That means that when you want to say "it is," you can use the word *it's*, with the apostrophe. When you want to show that something belongs to "it," use the word *its*, without the apostrophe.

It's going to be a quiet concert.
The band has lost *its* speakers.

When to Use an Apostrophe: Whose versus Who's, Theirs versus There's, Your versus You're

Once you understand the difference between a contraction and a possessive pronoun, you can easily figure out when to use the word with the apostrophe (the contraction) and when to use the other word (the possessive).

To choose whose versus who's, ask yourself if you can substitute the words *who is*. If you can, use *who's*. If not, use *whose*.

I know _____ playing that loud guitar.
I know *who is* playing that loud guitar.
Yes, use *who's*.
I know *who's* playing that loud guitar.

_____ orange sneakers are those?
Who is orange sneakers are those?
No, doesn't make sense. Use *whose*.
Whose orange sneakers are those?

To choose theirs versus there's, ask yourself if you can substitute the words *there is*. If you can, use *there's*. If not, use *theirs*.

_____ my best friend in the world.
There is my best friend in the world.
Yes, use *there's*.
There's my best friend in the world.

The best players are _____ .
The best players are *there is*. No, that's silly.
Use *theirs*.
The best players are *theirs*.

To choose your versus you're, ask yourself if you can substitute the words *you are*. If you can, use *you're*. If not, use *your*.

I hope _____ kidding!
I hope *you are* kidding! Yes, use *you're*.
I hope *you're* kidding!

Where is _____ spaceship?
Where is *you are* spaceship? That doesn't work.
Use *your*.
Where is *your* spaceship?

Remember: The apostrophe stands for the letter that has been left out.

who is	there is	you are
who'X̶s	there'X̶s	you'X̶re

106

Chapter 26:
Other Punctuation
(The Last Word)

Using Question Marks

This may be the easiest punctuation mark you ever have to use. It's simple: Use a *question mark* at the end of a question.

Did you ever hear of anything so easy?

Using Exclamation Points

This is almost as easy as using question marks. Use an *exclamation point* after an expression of feeling.

Don't touch that dial!

You can use an exclamation point after a single word.

Hey! Wow! Gee! Stop!

In many sentences, you would be equally correct using either a period or an exclamation point. It all depends on the feeling you want to convey. Just be careful not to use too many exclamation points. Overusing exclamation points is like raising your voice—it's more effective when you choose your moment carefully.

Using Colons

A *colon* introduces a list of items. Only use a colon after a complete sentence.

> I want you to get the following items from the store: bread, butter, and tomatoes.

A colon can also show the relationship of two thoughts:

> There was only one thing missing: the will to win.

If a complete sentence follows a colon, you have the option of starting it with a capital letter.

> Remember this: The will to win is all you need.

Using Dashes and Parentheses

These punctuation marks set off ideas that are not closely related to the main sentence. *Parentheses* can enclose a complete, separate sentence. *Dashes* can only be used inside a sentence.

> The team—which had not practiced since Sunday—was doing badly.

> The team was doing badly. (They had not practiced since Sunday.)

> The team was doing badly—but what else could you expect? They had not practiced since Sunday.

As you can see, dashes are more dramatic and tend to emphasize the information they set off. Parentheses tend to hide information. Use both types of punctuation sparingly, for emphasis. Using them too often becomes dull.

Using Semicolons

A *semicolon* has two main uses. One is to separate the main clauses in a compound sentence. A semicolon is necessary if the clauses are not joined by a coordinating conjunction such as *and, but, yet,* and *for*. A semicolon is also necessary if the clauses are joined by such words as *however, also, besides, indeed, otherwise, nonetheless, thus,* and *then*. Use a semicolon before those words and a comma after them.

No conjunction: We were hungry; we wanted to eat.

Conjunction: We were hungry; nevertheless, we waited for you.

The other main use of a semicolon is to separate long items in a list, especially if the items include commas of their own.

The flags' colors include red, white, and blue; black, green, and yellow; and a simple red and white.

Using Quotation Marks

Quotation marks are used to show someone's exact words. These exact words are known as a *quotation*.

She said, "I hope you're coming to my party tonight."

Many people get confused about which punctuation goes inside quotation marks and which goes outside. If a punctuation mark, such as an exclamation point or a question mark, is part of the quote, put it inside the quotation marks. For punctuation that is not part of the original quote, here are the rules.

Inside	Outside

commas
  "Come here," she
  said.
	semicolons
	  She said, "Come
	  here"; did she
	  mean it?

periods
  She said, "Come
  here."
	colons
	  She could only
	  remember the first
	  three words of "The
	  Cat and the
	  Fiddle": "Hey,
	  diddle diddle."

For a quote within a quote, use single quotation marks. "I heard her say 'Don't go!' to her father," explained Fred.

Quotation Marks versus Italics

There are two kinds of punctuation for titles: quotation marks and *italics*, a kind of type that slants.

When you are writing or typing, you cannot use the kind of italics that are printed in a book, so underline the words instead.

Italics or Underlining	*Quotation Marks*

the name of a book
    Dr. Zhivago
	the name of a short story or a poem
	    ''The Scarlet Ibis''
	    ''The Bells''

the name of an opera or long musical work
    Don Giovanni
	the name of a song
	    ''Yesterday''

the name of a magazine or newspaper
    The New York Times
    Popular Mechanics
	the title of an article
	    ''How to Fix a Carburetor''

the name of a television series
    Star Trek
	the name of an individual show in a series
	    ''The Captain's Revenge''

the name of a play or movie
    West Side Story
    Friday the Thirteenth	

As you can see, italics are used for bigger works, and quotation marks are used for smaller works.

Index